THE DOCTRINE

OF

AI GOVERNANCE

DR AMANYI VINCENT

ISBN:

Ebook: 978-1-971141-38-1

Paperback: 978-1-971141-36-7

Hardcover: 978-1-971141-37-4

Published by Columbus Book Publishers

www.columbusbookpublishers.com

Printed in the United States of America

DEDICATION

I dedicate this book to my late spouse, Deborah Amanyi, and to my sons—Dave, Darius, and Darien, who have given me the greatest honor of being their father.

INTRODUCTION

AI governance is not a new concept, it has evolved alongside the advancement and widespread adoption of AI technologies. In its early stages, governance was often overlooked due to AI's experimental nature. However, as the potential impacts and implications of AI became clear, the need for structured governance became critical.

Today, AI governance is increasingly shaped by a growing body of frameworks, legislation, and regulations designed to ensure the responsible development, deployment, and oversight of AI systems. AI technologies are now embedded across business functions—from decision-making algorithms to customer service chatbots. Without robust governance structures, these tools risk perpetuating bias, compromising privacy, and eroding public trust. Yet, countless data governance decisions occur beyond the international sphere, such as crafting guidance by sector regulators, selecting training data for chatbot fine-tuning, and deploying data-driven systems in schools and workplaces. AI governance is a set of rules and processes that guide how AI systems are built and used responsibly. It makes sure these systems are clear, explainable, and accountable. It also helps reduce risks and prevent harmful mistakes or biases in AI models.

The ethical implications of AI are too significant to ignore. For example, algorithmic bias can lead to discriminatory outcomes in hiring, lending, and law enforcement. These challenges are compounded by data privacy concerns, where personal information may be mishandled or exploited. The purpose of AI governance is to ensure that the benefits of machine learning and other AI technologies are accessible to everyone in a fair and equitable manner. It promotes ethical AI use by making its application transparent, safe, private, accountable, and free from bias. Data governance involves setting and overseeing rules for how data is collected, used, and shared, decisions that directly shape the design and functioning of AI systems. These decisions can occur at global, regional, national, and local levels, including within individual organizations.

One of today's most pressing challenges is the overwhelming volume of data generated by AI systems. As data inventories expand rapidly, mechanisms for cleansing and organizing this information often lag behind. Companies are accumulating vast datasets, yet critical processes to ensure accuracy, consistency, and relevance are frequently neglected. Without proper data cleansing, organizations risk relying on flawed or outdated information—leading to poor decisions, distorted insights, and diminished customer trust. Machine learning identifies patterns within large volumes of training data to make predictions, offer recommendations, and, with the advent of generative

AI, create entirely new content. The type, amount, and quality of this training data strongly influence an AI system's capabilities and the biases it may reproduce.

In addition, the absence of robust governance structures exposes organizations to legal liabilities and operational risks. Neglecting ethical AI practices not only puts CEOs at risk of regulatory non-compliance but also threatens the long-term sustainability of businesses in a marketplace that increasingly values ethical leadership. Although some governments have begun drafting regulations to address these concerns, legislative progress remains far too slow to keep pace with the rapid evolution of AI technology. We cannot afford to wait for governments to catch up. As leaders, we must take a proactive approach to AI governance—implementing frameworks and strategies now rather than relying on external regulations to dictate our actions.

The ethical implications of AI demand that businesses lead the way in creating responsible and transparent systems. Embedding AI governance into corporate strategy not only mitigates legal and reputational risks but also fosters sustainable, responsible innovation. A strong commitment to ethical AI enables companies to remain competitive, build lasting trust with stakeholders, and make a positive societal impact.

Conversely, neglecting AI governance carries significant risks. Beyond potential regulatory fines, the reputational damage from a poorly managed AI system can be severe. The challenge spans every discipline, organizational, ethical, and strategic. Companies are racing to deploy AI, yet most lack robust frameworks for accountability, data integrity, and sustainable value creation. AI systems evolve faster than governance can keep pace, sharpening the tension between innovation and control with every passing quarter.

AI introduces profound ethical challenges, from algorithmic bias to autonomous decision-making that demand more than reactive measures. To be effective, regulation and governance must be principle-driven and risk-based, anchored in transparency, fairness, privacy, adaptability, and accountability. Addressing these issues through robust governance mechanisms is essential to building trust in AI systems. The goal isn't static compliance; it's dynamic governance that evolves with technology. Achieving this requires frameworks that are not only strong but flexible, capable of operating at company, sovereign, and global levels. Organizations that lead in governance will lead in innovation, securing both trust and competitive advantage in an AI-driven economy. Great tech firms have faced penalties for failing to meet data privacy standards, but the greater cost lies in the erosion of public trust. Once issues such as biased algorithms, data breaches, or a lack of transparency arise, rebuilding that trust becomes an uphill battle. Establishing and maintaining an AI governance framework enables organizations to ensure responsible, ethical, and compliant use of AI. Over time, this approach strengthens customer trust, mitigates risks, and maximizes business value. There is an increasing need to establish a strong governance framework to effectively manage emerging capabilities, with well-defined guardrails to mitigate potential issues. However, the organization has been slow to adopt governance, largely because it is waiting for government institutions to finalize and harmonize regulations and policies. These policies are expected to enable capabilities without compromising value creation or introducing liability risks. AI is no longer a distant promise, it's transforming the way we work, make decisions, and compete today. Customer service relies on it. Code generation thrives on it. Drug discovery accelerates because of it. Across every industry, AI systems have become integral to daily operations. Yet for organizations, a critical challenge is emerging on how to govern these systems responsibly while unlocking their full potential.

TABLE OF CONTENTS

GOVERNANCE ENABLEMENT

A governance framework, also known as a governance structure, is essential for modern governance and legal operations. It establishes how individuals interact with the organization, regulators, and stakeholders, providing clear guidance for managing and monitoring operations. It's time to debunk the myth that more data automatically means better AI.

The truth is, quantity without quality can cripple your AI initiatives. Incomplete, inaccurate, or siloed data doesn't just slow progress, it sabotages results, no matter how advanced your algorithms are. Yet many organizations dive into AI projects without a solid data strategy, setting themselves up for failure. If you want AI to deliver real, actionable insights, start with the foundation: data that is organized, accurate, and timely. Without it, even the smartest AI can't perform.

AI governance focuses on the responsible development, deployment, and oversight of artificial intelligence systems. Its goal is to ensure that AI operates ethically, transparently, fairly, securely, and in alignment with legal and organizational values. AI governance consists of multiple interconnected layers, from organizational structure to regulatory compliance. It involves implementing standardized governance practices and regulatory frameworks to guide the development and deployment of AI technologies. Information cleanup isn't a *"one-and-done"* task, it's an ongoing commitment.

As organizations grow, their data landscape constantly changes. To keep information organized and reliable, regular monitoring, updates, and audits are non-negotiable. Data governance must be woven into the fabric of the organizational culture, backed by clear accountability and well-defined roles.

The first step is to raise awareness of the new challenges and risks introduced by AI. As AI becomes more prevalent in public discourse and workplace conversations, many individuals may already be aware of these risks, some with concerns, strong opinions, or even fears about an AI-driven future. The shift from data chaos to order isn't just about streamlining operations, it's about unlocking transformative opportunities. A well-structured information ecosystem empowers organizations to make confident, data-driven decisions, deliver personalized customer experiences, and spark innovation by revealing hidden patterns and trends. The first step to making data and AI governance fair is explaining why it's important. Many people think involving those affected by technology is about fairness, but it also brings clear benefits. These include lowering risks, helping rules adapt as technology changes, and building public trust so AI can be used safely and widely.

A key consideration is aligning governance with varying levels of AI risk. For example, applications with minimal impact on people may require little or no oversight, while those directly affecting individuals, such as AI in hiring or financial lending, and especially high-impact uses like healthcare decision-making, demand a tiered, risk-based governance approach. If you're in a leadership role, start by engaging your peers across the organization. Build buy-in by clearly outlining what you need from them and the outcomes you aim to achieve. For example:

- Review new and existing AI use cases for potential risks

- Ensure policy alignment across all functions

- Assign clear ownership for oversight

- Share updates on emerging regulatory developments and assess their impact across the organization.

The first critical step in developing an AI governance framework is defining your organization's goals. The framework's objectives and scope should be clear and aligned with business priorities, regulatory requirements, and broader risk management strategies. By setting well-defined objectives, your team can ensure that AI governance initiatives foster innovation while maintaining compliance and trust. After defining the objectives and scope of your framework, the next step is to establish policies and standards that ensure AI systems operate ethically, securely, and in full compliance with regulations. AI risk refers to the unique vulnerabilities an organization assumes when adopting artificial intelligence. A structured AI risk management process helps identify potential pitfalls early and proactively address them to mitigate risks. Because AI risks evolve over time, the framework should include continuous monitoring for emerging risks and ongoing compliance.

AI governance is not the responsibility of a single department, it requires collaboration across cross-functional teams to build and maintain trustworthy AI systems. Executive leadership should take the lead, with legal, engineering, cybersecurity, and risk management teams aligned and working toward the same objectives. Governance without ownership leads to chaos. Every organization needs a clear answer to one critical question: Who is responsible for monitoring AI-related risks? If that role or team doesn't exist yet, bring decision-makers together and define it, because without ownership, progress stalls and critical decisions remain unresolved. One effective approach is to establish a steering committee. This doesn't have to be large or overly formal; a small, cross-functional group that meets regularly can make a big impact. Their mandate? Evaluate risks, guide policy, and track adoption, embedding accountability into the heart of your AI strategy.

DEVELOP AI GOVERNANCE TEAM

The next step is to establish an AI governance team responsible for overseeing the governance framework. This team should be intentionally cross-disciplinary, with representation from all major areas of the business.

Below are examples of roles and responsibilities that can contribute to building an effective AI governance structure.

LEGAL AND COMPLIANCE

This function is accountable for interpreting and applying laws, regulations, and contractual obligations governing AI systems. It ensures full adherence to legal and regulatory standards while collaborating closely with privacy and cybersecurity teams to design, implement, and enforce comprehensive AI policies.

These policies encompass critical areas such as acceptable use, data sharing protocols, and AI model governance to maintain compliance and mitigate risk across the enterprise.

Purpose: To ensure that all AI systems and related processes comply with applicable laws, regulations, and contractual obligations, while mitigating legal and regulatory risks through robust governance frameworks and policy enforcement.

Interpret and Apply Regulatory Requirements: Continuously monitor and interpret evolving laws, regulations, and contractual obligations related to AI systems, ensuring timely compliance.

Develop and Enforce AI Governance Policies: Collaborate with privacy and cybersecurity teams to design, implement, and enforce policies covering acceptable use, data sharing, and AI model governance.

Ensure Contractual and Ethical Compliance: Validate that AI deployments adhere to contractual terms and ethical standards, reducing exposure to legal liabilities.

Integrate Compliance into AI Lifecycle: Embed compliance checkpoints throughout the AI development and deployment lifecycle, from data acquisition to model deployment and monitoring.

Maintain Regulatory Readiness:

Prepare for audits and regulatory reviews by maintaining accurate documentation and evidence of compliance activities.

CYBERSECURITY

This function is accountable for ensuring the integrity and resilience of AI systems across the enterprise. Key responsibilities include implementing and maintaining robust access controls, monitoring data flows, and securing third-party APIs as well as internet-facing services. Additionally, the role encompasses advanced threat detection, coordinated incident response, and comprehensive vulnerability management to safeguard all AI environments against emerging risks.

Purpose: To ensure the integrity, confidentiality, and resilience of AI systems across the enterprise by implementing robust security measures and proactive risk management practices.

Establish Comprehensive Security Controls: Implement and maintain enterprise-grade access controls, encryption standards, and secure integration protocols for AI systems.

Monitor and Protect AI Ecosystem: Continuously monitor data flows, third-party APIs, and internet-facing services to prevent unauthorized access and mitigate potential vulnerabilities.

Enhance Threat Detection and Response: Develop advanced threat detection capabilities and maintain a coordinated incident response framework to address security breaches promptly.

Implement Vulnerability Management Program: Conduct regular vulnerability assessments and remediation activities to ensure AI environments remain secure against emerging risks.

Align with Regulatory and Governance Standards: Ensure all security practices comply with internal governance policies and external regulatory requirements.

HUMAN RESOURCES (HR)

This function is responsible for developing and enforcing AI-related workforce policies, including acceptable use guidelines, while proactively managing organizational and employee impacts. HR also designs and delivers comprehensive training programs to enhance AI literacy and promote responsible adoption across all levels of the organization.

Purpose: To manage the workforce implications of AI adoption by establishing clear policies, fostering organizational readiness, and equipping employees with the skills and knowledge required for responsible and ethical AI use.

Develop and Enforce Workforce Policies: Create and maintain AI-related policies, including acceptable use guidelines, to ensure responsible integration of AI technologies across the organization.

Manage Workforce Impact and Change: Implement strategies to address workforce transitions, role evolution, and employee engagement resulting from AI adoption.

Design and Deliver AI Literacy Programs: Develop comprehensive training programs to build AI literacy and awareness, ensuring employees understand both opportunities and risks.

Promote Ethical and Responsible AI Use: Embed ethical considerations into HR practices, ensuring employees adhere to governance principles and organizational values.

Support Continuous Learning and Upskilling: Establish ongoing learning pathways to prepare employees for emerging AI-related roles and responsibilities.

FINANCE

This function is accountable for overseeing financial planning and resource allocation for AI initiatives. Responsibilities include managing budgets for AI tools and services, evaluating return on investment (ROI), and assessing financial risks and cost implications associated with AI adoption across all business operations.

Purpose: To ensure the financial sustainability and strategic allocation of resources for AI initiatives by managing budgets, evaluating return on investment (ROI), and mitigating financial risks associated with AI adoption across the enterprise.

Establish AI Budgeting Framework: Develop and maintain a structured budgeting process for AI tools, services, and infrastructure to support organizational priorities.

Evaluate Financial Performance and ROI: Implement robust methodologies to measure the return on investment for AI projects and ensure alignment with business objectives.

Assess Financial Risks and Cost Implications: Identify and mitigate financial risks, including cost overruns, vendor dependencies, and long-term operational expenses.

Optimize Resource Allocation: Ensure efficient allocation of financial and operational resources to maximize value and minimize waste across AI initiatives.

Enable Transparent Financial Governance: Maintain clear reporting and accountability mechanisms for AI-related expenditures to support audit readiness and stakeholder confidence.

INFORMATION TECHNOLOGY

This function is responsible for overseeing enterprise infrastructure, cloud environments, and AI data platforms, ensuring that all systems supporting AI services are secure, reliable, scalable, and highly available.

Purpose: To ensure the reliability, scalability, security, and high availability of all infrastructure components, cloud environments, and AI data platforms that support enterprise AI services. This function provides the technical foundation for sustainable AI operations and aligns infrastructure capabilities with organizational governance standards.

Maintain Robust Infrastructure for AI Services: Ensure enterprise infrastructure and cloud environments are optimized for performance, resilience, and scalability to support AI workloads.

Secure AI Platforms and Environments: Implement advanced security measures across all AI data platforms, including encryption, access controls, and continuous monitoring.

Enable High Availability and Disaster Recovery: Design and maintain systems that guarantee uptime and provide comprehensive disaster recovery capabilities for AI services.

Optimize Resource Utilization: Monitor and manage infrastructure resources to achieve cost efficiency without compromising reliability or performance.

Support Continuous Innovation and Integration: Ensure infrastructure readiness for emerging AI technologies and seamless integration with enterprise systems.

PRIVACY

This function is responsible for managing the collection, use, disclosure, and retention of personal data, sensitive information, proprietary content, and intellectual property. It works in close collaboration with cybersecurity and legal teams to ensure full compliance with privacy regulations and organizational data-handling policies.

Purpose: To ensure the ethical, secure, and compliant management of data throughout the AI lifecycle by establishing robust governance practices for the collection, use, disclosure, and retention of personal data, sensitive information, proprietary content, and intellectual property.

Implement Comprehensive Data Governance Framework: Define and enforce policies governing data collection, usage, sharing, and retention to align with organizational standards and regulatory requirements.

Ensure Privacy and Regulatory Compliance: Collaborate with legal and cybersecurity teams to maintain compliance with global privacy laws and internal data-handling policies.

Protect Sensitive and Proprietary Information: Establish controls to safeguard intellectual property and sensitive data against unauthorized access and misuse.

Enable Data Transparency and Accountability: Maintain clear documentation and audit trails for all AI-related data activities to support regulatory reviews and internal audits.

Support Ethical AI Development: Embed principles of fairness, transparency, and responsible data use into AI model development and deployment processes.

BUSINESS UNITS

Represent core functional and strategic priorities by defining and continuously refining AI use cases that align with organizational objectives and operational requirements.

Purpose: To ensure AI initiatives reflect core functional and strategic priorities by defining, validating, and refining AI use cases that align with organizational objectives and operational requirements.

Represent Strategic and Functional Priorities: Act as the voice of business units to guarantee AI solutions address real operational needs and strategic goals.

Define and Validate AI Use Cases: Identify high-value AI opportunities and validate feasibility, impact, and alignment with governance principles.

Refine Use Cases Continuously: Establish an iterative process for reviewing and updating AI use cases based on evolving business requirements and technological advancements.

Ensure Cross-Functional Collaboration: Facilitate engagement between technical teams and business stakeholders to ensure clarity, transparency, and shared accountability.

Measure Business Impact of AI Initiatives: Track and report on the effectiveness of AI solutions in delivering measurable business outcomes.

OPERATIONS

This function ensures that AI systems deliver operational efficiency, reliability, and resilience across the enterprise. It is also responsible for overseeing change management processes to enable the seamless integration of AI into existing workflows and business operations.

Purpose: To ensure AI systems deliver operational efficiency, reliability, and resilience while enabling seamless integration into existing workflows and processes through structured change management practices.

Drive Operational Efficiency and Reliability: Optimize AI-enabled processes to improve productivity, reduce errors, and enhance overall system performance.

Ensure Business Continuity and Resilience: Implement strategies that maintain operational stability during AI deployment and minimize disruption to critical services.

Oversee Change Management for AI Integration: Develop and execute change management plans that facilitate smooth adoption of AI technologies across business units.

Promote Stakeholder Engagement and Communication: Establish clear communication channels and training programs to prepare employees for process changes and new workflows.

Monitor and Evaluate AI Operational Impact: Continuously assess the effectiveness of AI systems in achieving operational goals and refine processes based on performance data.

EXECUTIVE LEADERSHIP

Provides strategic direction and oversight for AI initiatives, establishes organizational risk appetite, ensures alignment with enterprise priorities, allocates resources effectively, and champions AI governance at the board level.

Purpose: To provide strategic direction and oversight for AI initiatives, establish organizational risk appetite, ensure alignment with enterprise priorities, allocate resources effectively, and advocate for AI governance at the highest levels of leadership.

Define Strategic Vision for AI Governance: Set the long-term vision and priorities for AI adoption and governance, ensuring alignment with enterprise strategy.

Establish Risk Appetite and Tolerance: Determine acceptable levels of risk for AI initiatives and ensure governance frameworks reflect these thresholds.

Ensure Enterprise Alignment: Validate that all AI programs and governance activities support organizational objectives and deliver measurable business value.

Allocate Resources and Funding: Approve and oversee resource allocation for AI governance, including financial, technological, and human capital investments.

Advocate for Governance at Board Level: Champion AI governance principles and compliance requirements in executive and board discussions to secure ongoing support.

AI GOVERNANCE BEST PRACTICE

A common challenge—particularly within privacy and security functions—is the expectation to address every issue, including those outside their scope, such as matters more appropriately managed by business, legal, or HR teams. Reluctance to collaborate across functions often arises from delayed responses to inquiries. In some cases, this is compounded by an organizational culture that lacks robust information-sharing practices among trusted peers, and by the absence of formal processes designed to facilitate cross-functional collaboration.

AI is rapidly becoming pervasive, integrated into nearly every process and system across the enterprise. Its influence extends to every function and individual. While AI is transforming business operations, only organizations that proactively govern its use will fully capture its benefits. In the absence of governance, AI introduces significant, unmanaged, and unmitigated risks.

Define and Develop AI Use Cases: Create and refine AI use cases for enterprise-wide implementation and targeted functional applications to ensure alignment with organizational objectives.

Ensure Fairness and Bias Mitigation: Validate that AI-generated analyses and outputs are as free from bias as possible, promoting ethical and equitable outcomes.

Monitor Model Performance: Continuously track AI models for performance drift and deviations from expected behavior, implementing corrective measures when necessary.

Maintain Human Oversight: Ensure a "human-in-the-loop" approach for high-risk use cases or scenarios requiring human judgment, values, or discernment.

Select and Vet AI Solutions: Evaluate and approve AI tools and services to ensure quality, compliance, and alignment with organizational standards.

Develop and Enforce AI Policies: Establish governance policies—such as acceptable use guidelines—to promote responsible and secure AI practices.

Design and Deliver AI Literacy Programs: Provide comprehensive training to build workforce AI literacy and ensure responsible adoption across all levels.

Prepare Workforce for AI Integration: Implement change management strategies to enable effective adoption and utilization of AI solutions and services.

Optimize Workforce Use of AI Capabilities: Ensure employees leverage AI solutions efficiently, including agentic AI (autonomous task agents), generative AI (e.g., large language models), and other advanced technologies.

Facilitate Continuous Feedback: Collect and incorporate feedback to strengthen and evolve AI governance practices across the organization.

GOOD PRIVACY PRACTICES FOR RESPONSIBLE AI GOVERNANCE

Establishing strong data privacy practices creates a solid foundation for building an effective AI governance program. Think of a privacy management platform as the foundation of a house and AI governance as the architectural blueprint.

When the foundation is strong and level, constructing a safe, stable structure becomes far easier. Similarly, a robust privacy framework simplifies and strengthens AI governance because the essential rules, boundaries, and safeguards are already in place to support responsible implementation.

Develop and clearly articulate internal and external policies, ensuring they are accessible to regulators and stakeholders. These frameworks should serve as a blueprint for creating additional governance policies. It is essential to harmonize all relevant policies to establish a robust governance structure. Implement processes to discover and track data across the organization to understand where and how personal and sensitive information is being used, including within AI tools and projects. Additionally, assess how third parties manage data, particularly in the context of AI, to ensure compliance and mitigate risk.

Communicate clearly and consistently across the organization to align on AI usage and risk management practices. Once policies governing personal and sensitive data are established, ensure visibility into where this data resides, how it is used, and the associated operational risks. This transparency enables stronger protection of personal and sensitive information in every context. Ultimately, robust privacy governance serves as the foundation for effective AI governance.

To promote responsible and ethical practices throughout the AI system lifecycle, organizations must make informed decisions during development, deployment, and monitoring to ensure systems perform as intended. Effective AI governance incorporates oversight mechanisms that address risks such as bias, privacy infringement, and misuse, while fostering innovation and building trust. A structured governance approach provides assurance that these risks are mitigated. One critical enabler is the establishment of comprehensive AI policies and procedures. Defining roles, responsibilities, and clear expectations creates essential guardrails that shape how individuals approach and utilize AI responsibly.

RECOMMENDED BEST PRACTICES

Identify Current AI Usage: Conduct a comprehensive assessment to determine where AI is currently deployed within the organization, encouraging transparency to uncover hidden or unauthorized uses.

Establish Robust AI Policies and Procedures: Develop clear policies that define roles, responsibilities, and governance guardrails to ensure consistent and responsible AI practices.

Deliver AI Literacy and Policy Training: Provide mandatory training programs to build foundational AI knowledge and ensure workforce understanding of organizational policies and procedures.

Monitor and Enforce Policy Compliance: Implement mechanisms to track adherence to AI policies and take prompt corrective action in cases of noncompliance.

Monitor AI Tools and Systems: Continuously evaluate AI systems for performance, security, and ethical compliance, addressing issues proactively.

Ensure Regulatory Compliance: Comply with all applicable legislation related to data protection, AI systems, intellectual property, confidentiality, and breach reporting.

Maintain Comprehensive Documentation: Ensure accurate and complete documentation of AI systems, policies, and governance activities to support audits and accountability.

CONCLUSION

The challenge of AI governance centers on timing and integration. The most effective approach balances speed with scrutiny—accelerating where risks are minimal and applying caution where consequences are significant. Without a strong data foundation, AI integration can fail to deliver value and may even undermine business performance. Small oversights can escalate quickly: outdated information surfaces during urgent searches, irrelevant content clouds critical decisions, and operational efficiency declines. When systems are cluttered with stale data, AI amplifies the noise instead of cutting through it. To unlock AI's full potential, leaders must prioritize clean, current, and connected data as the cornerstone of governance.

The cost of inaction extends beyond inefficiency—it results in lost competitive advantage. AI governance is not a choice between innovation and control; it is about creating an environment where both accelerate together. For organizations, this means embedding governance into the core of AI adoption rather than treating it as an afterthought.

Strong data foundations, clear accountability frameworks, disciplined change management, and adaptive leadership are the pillars that make this possible. Far from slowing progress, these elements act as catalysts: they reduce risk, build trust, and enable AI to scale faster and smarter. Organizations that invest in governance early avoid costly missteps and position themselves to achieve sustainable competitive advantage in an AI-driven economy.

I. **Governance is a Growth Enabler**: It accelerates innovation while managing risk.

II. **Data is the Foundation:** Clean, current, and connected data underpins every successful AI initiative.

III. **Policies Provide Guardrails:** Clear roles, responsibilities, and accountability frameworks ensure ethical and compliant AI use.

IV. **Leadership Drives Success:** Executive commitment and cross-functional collaboration are essential for governance maturity.

V. **Early Investment Pays Off:** Organizations that embed governance from the start gain trust, resilience, and competitive advantage.

To transform governance from a static, periodic checkpoint into a dynamic, continuous safeguard by integrating compliance directly into AI workflows. This approach ensures transparency, accountability, and risk mitigation without slowing innovation, enabling organizations to scale AI responsibly and confidently.

CORE PRINCIPLES

A. Governance by Design

Embed compliance and risk controls into AI systems from inception, ensuring governance is integral—not an afterthought.

B. Automation and Integration

Leverage automated compliance checks and embedded audit trails within AI workflows to maintain transparency without disrupting operations.

C. Risk-Based Agility

Accelerate deployment where risks are minimal and apply heightened scrutiny where consequences are significant.

D. Real-Time Monitoring

Continuously monitor AI performance, data usage, and compliance indicators to detect and address issues proactively.

E. Transparency and Accountability

Ensure every AI process includes traceable decision-making and clear documentation to support audits and stakeholder trust.

F. Culture of Continuous Improvement

Foster collaboration across teams to refine governance practices as technology and regulations evolve.

www.ingramcontent.com/pod-product-compliance
Lightning Source LLC
Chambersburg PA
CBHW052352030726
47602CB00002B/25